W9-BYK-768

Bill Clinton

Bill Clinton

Sean McCollum

Library Media Center
Gregoc Middle School
2621 Springdale Circle
Naperville, IL 60564

AMERICA'S

42ND

PRESIDENT

Children's Press®
A Division of Scholastic Inc.
New York / Toronto / London / Auckland / Sydney
Mexico City / New Delhi / Hong Kong
Danbury, Connecticut

Library of Congress Cataloging-in-Publication Data

McCollum, Sean.
    Bill Clinton / Sean McCollum.
      p. cm. — (Encyclopedia of presidents. Second series)
    Includes bibliographical references and index.
  ISBN 0-516-22980-X
   1. Clinton, Bill, 1946–   —Juvenile literature. 2. Presidents—United
States—Biography—Juvenile literature. I. Title. II. Series: Encyclopedia of
presidents (2003)

  E886.M355 2005
  973.929'092—dc22   2004020433

© 2005 by Sean McCollum
All rights reserved. Published in 2005 by Children's Press, an imprint of
Scholastic Library Publishing.
Published simultaneously in Canada.
Printed in the United States of America.

CHILDREN'S PRESS and associated logos are trademarks and or registered
trademarks of Scholastic Library Publishing. SCHOLASTIC and associated
logos are trademarks and or registered trademarks of Scholastic Inc.
1 2 3 4 5 6 7 8 9 10 R 14 13 12 11 10 09 08 07 06 05

Contents

Chapter 1

Meeting a President ────────────

Boys Nation had been meeting in hot and humid Washington, D.C., for nearly a week. As part of a program sponsored by the American Legion, two teenage boys from each state imitated the U.S. Senate, debating government policy, forming coalitions, and voting on imaginary bills. They also visited historical sites and gained introductions to real political leaders. Meanwhile, the real U.S. government chugged and churned all around them.

The highlight of the trip came on July 24, 1963, when two air-conditioned buses carried the boys to the White House. They assembled in the Rose Garden. Soon President John F. Kennedy emerged from the Oval Office. He congratulated the boys and made some remarks. Kennedy turned to head back to his office, but he unexpectedly circled back to shake hands. The boys surged forward. The long

High school student Bill Clinton shakes hands with President John F. Kennedy in July 1963.

legs of one 16-year-old boy from Arkansas—already six-foot-three (1.91 meters)—got him there first. He shook Kennedy's hand as a photographer took their picture. It showed President Kennedy with a young man who would follow in his footsteps 30 years later. The Arkansas boy was Bill Clinton. He later pointed to that meeting as one of his inspirations for going into politics and public service.

Billy Blythe

On May 17, 1946, salesman Bill Blythe began the long drive from Chicago, Illinois, to Hope, Arkansas, to pick up his young, pregnant wife. Blythe, a young World War II veteran, never reached Hope. A tire blew out, his car flipped, and he was found drowned in a water-filled ditch. Three months later, on August 19, Virginia Cassidy Blythe gave birth to a son and named him William Jefferson Blythe IV.

The future seemed uncertain for the young single mom and her baby. Still, young Billy was surrounded by devotion—and orneriness—from his mother and her parents. His boyhood was filled with emotional drama and family difficulties, as well as top personal achievement. Even as a boy, he exhibited some of the talents and character that would aid his rise to the U.S. presidency.

Not long after Billy Blythe was born, his mother moved to New Orleans to train as a nurse. She left Billy with his grandparents, Edith and Eldridge Cassidy, who adored the boy. Edith, whom Billy called "Mammaw," took firm control of the boy's life. A nurse with a fierce temper, she sternly managed Billy's eating, sleep, and preschool education. "My high chair faced the window," Bill Clinton recalled in his autobiography, *My Life*, "and Mammaw tacked playing cards up on the wooden window frame at mealtimes so that I could learn to count." She often read to him, and Billy was reading by himself at age three.

Billy received a different kind of education from "Pappaw," a man he remembered as "the kindest person" he ever knew. Eldridge Cassidy owned a small grocery store on the edge of "Colored Town," where Hope's African Americans lived. In Arkansas at that time, relations between whites and blacks were terrible. By tradition and law, blacks were forced to go to separate schools and use separate public restrooms, swimming pools, restaurants, and hotels.

At the Cassidy store, though, white and black customers mingled. Eldridge sold goods and extended credit to everyone. Outside the store, his grandson played with black and white kids alike. This early experience stuck with Billy, and he grew up free of racial prejudices. Years later, a black leader referred to him as "the first black president" because of his fellow feeling with African Americans.

In 1950, when Billy was four, his mom returned to Hope and reclaimed her son. In the years to come, she would become the biggest and most positive influence in his life. A year after she returned to Hope, Virginia married Roger Clinton. Clinton owned a car dealership. He and Virginia enjoyed partying together, and both loved to gamble. Billy's grandparents were against the marriage and even prevented him from attending the wedding. Soon their doubts about Roger Clinton proved to be well founded. He was a poor businessman and a compulsive gambler. Worse, he was an alcoholic who could become mean and abusive when he was drinking.

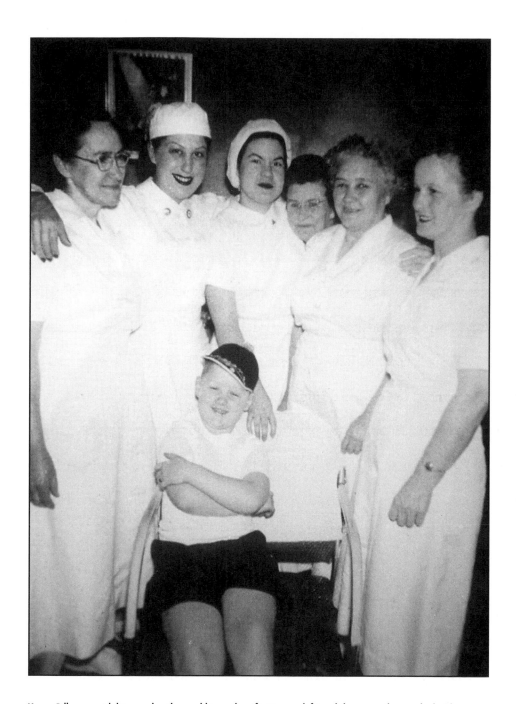

Young Bill poses with his grandmother and his mother (first two on left) and the nurses they worked with.

Before long, young Billy had to listen to the terrible sounds of his new stepfather threatening and yelling at his mom. Once when Bill was five, Roger pulled out a gun and fired a bullet into the wall to scare Virginia. Roger was arrested and dragged off to jail for the night. "It really was a painful experience to see someone you love . . . that you care about just in the grip of a demon," Clinton remarked later about his stepfather and his alcoholism.

A year later, the family moved from Hope to Hot Springs, Arkansas, a resort city at the edge of Hot Springs National Park. Bill would grow up in Hot Springs and achieve an early reputation for achievement. He was known to all as Bill Clinton. His half brother, Roger Jr., was born there in 1956, when Bill was ten.

Even in elementary school, Bill seemed able to excel without having to study very hard. He was competitive, always striving to be the best in his class, but he was also polite and helpful and had a strong sense of virtue. Even though his mom and stepfather rarely went to church, Bill got up on Sunday, dressed in a suit, and went to the Baptist church by himself. Bill also loved to eat, and he was growing in a hurry. At 14 he was already nearly six feet (1.83 m) tall.

Roger Clinton's drinking and abusive behavior continued. Bill kept it a secret from even his closest friends, but it troubled him. One evening, he finally lost his patience. His parents were in their bedroom and Roger was hurling insults

In 1957, when Bill was eleven, the attention of the world focused on Little Rock, the Arkansas state capital. Three years earlier, the U.S. Supreme Court had ruled that separate schools for whites and African Americans were unconstitutional. Now Little Rock's Central High School had been ordered to desegregate, allowing nine black students to attend classes at the all-white school. When they came to register, however, the black students were turned away.

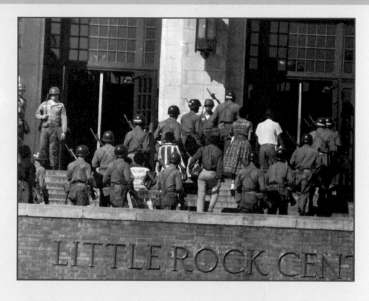

National Guard troops escort African American students into Little Rock's Central High School in the fall of 1957.

On September 23, they entered the building by a back way. A mob of nearly a thousand white people gathered outside, threatening the black students as they left the building. Finally, President Dwight D. Eisenhower ordered federal troops to protect the students as they entered and left school each day. One of the students, 15-year-old Minnijean Brown, said, "For the first time in my life, I feel like an American citizen."

Young Bill Clinton watched the drama on television. He later said he "felt somehow personally connected to those brave boys and girls as they marched through a mob right up to the front steps of Central High." As governor of Arkansas 30 years later, Clinton honored these first black students in a ceremony at the school. He said it was one of his proudest moments as governor.

☆ ☆ ☆

Bill Clinton, his mother, and his half brother Roger Clinton, about 1959.

and throwing punches at Virginia. "I grabbed a golf club out of my bag and threw open their door. Mother was on the floor and Daddy was standing over her, beating on her. I told him to stop and said that if he didn't I was going to beat the hell out of him with the golf club." For a while, the abuse stopped.

In later years, Clinton saw a silver lining to the family troubles he faced as a boy. He said they "gave me a high pain threshold, which, I think, is a very important thing to have in public life. You have to be able to take a lot of criticism—suffer defeats and get up tomorrow and fight again. And I think that my childhood had a lot to do with that."

Hotshot in Hot Springs ————————————————

In high school, Bill took the hardest courses and earned top grades, but he was regularly scolded for talking in class. "I could never keep my mouth shut," he said later. He became a student leader, serving as class president each of his first three years. He was active in public service organizations. Music was his special love, specifically band, where he played the tenor saxophone. He helped organize a cool jazz trio called "The Kingsmen."

Then came that fateful trip to Washington in the summer of 1963. Bill returned with the photograph of him shaking hands with President Kennedy and a fascination with the nation's capital city. "When he came back from Washington," his mother said later, "holding this picture of himself with Jack Kennedy, and the expression on his face, I knew right then that politics was the answer for him."

That November, Bill was sitting in trigonometry class when his teacher took a phone call, then returned with a stunned look on his face. "The president has been shot in Dallas," he said. Soon afterward, President Kennedy died.

"Ask not what your country can do for you. Ask what you can do for your country." With those words, John F. Kennedy ushered in his presidency in 1961.

Bill Clinton and many in his generation responded, inspired by the president's youthful energy. Kennedy's vision of landing a man on the moon captured the country's imagination and sparked the U.S. space program. His support of civil rights for black people moved many Americans of all races to join that struggle. His creation of the Peace Corps sent hundreds of young volunteers overseas to help in poor countries.

Nearly 30 years after John F. Kennedy's assassination, Bill Clinton visited Arlington National Cemetery to lay a rose on his hero's grave on the day before his own inauguration as president.

President John F. Kennedy, who inspired Bill Clinton and others of his generation.

☆ ☆ ☆

That same year, Bill took legal action to change his last name to Clinton, in spite of his difficult relationship with his stepfather. "I thought it was something I ought to do," he said later. "I thought it would be a gesture of family solidarity. And I thought it would be good for my brother."

Bill graduated 4th in his class of 363. In his yearbook, guidance counselor Edith Irons wrote: "Billy, I am honored to have known a gentleman who has courage, ambition, and determination."

Making Connections

After his visit to Washington for Boys Nation, Bill Clinton began to consider a career as a *diplomat* (an overseas representative of the government). His guidance counselor suggested Georgetown University in Washington, D.C. Pleased with the idea of returning to the nation's capital, Bill sent his only college application to Georgetown. He was accepted, and he enrolled for classes in September 1964.

Clinton was not the usual student in Georgetown's Edmund A. Walsh School of Foreign Service. He stood out as a small-town boy among the wealthy and worldly children of government officials, military officers, and lawyers. From the beginning, though, he was determined to succeed. The handsome freshman with the Arkansas drawl immediately ran for and won the office of freshman class president.

The campus of Georgetown University in Washington, D.C., where Clinton studied from 1964 to 1968.

Clinton continued his academic success, and he also began making useful connections in the political world. He spent the summer after his sophomore year in Arkansas, working on the campaign of a Democratic candidate for governor. The candidate lost, but Bill made contacts that helped him land a post in the Washington office of Arkansas senator J. William Fulbright. As a junior assistant, he stuffed envelopes and answered the phone, often working into the night. Fulbright was chairman of the Senate Foreign Relations Committee, and Clinton got an insider's view of hearings Fulbright held on the growing conflict in Vietnam. Fulbright was an early critic of the war, and Clinton's views were influenced by what he heard.

Clinton graduated from Georgetown in 1968. In his last year, he was selected to be a Rhodes Scholar, entitling him to study at Great Britain's famed Oxford University.

Dark Clouds Over Oxford ———————

In the fall of 1968, Bill Clinton and 31 other Rhodes Scholars arrived beneath the ancient spires of Oxford University. He soon wrote a letter to a friend describing his life there: "I read a lot, explore a lot, talk a lot to people from all over the world, try my hand at familiar and unfamiliar sports, take French lessons and an economic tutorial on the side, and attend a few lectures a week. The pace is much slower than I'm used to."

The slow pace gave Clinton time for a different kind of education. Surrounded by other quick and curious minds, Clinton talked, reasoned, argued, and explored ideas. He befriended Robert Reich, a brilliant young man who stood less than five feet (1.52 m) tall. The two were an odd pair as they walked across the campus deep in conversation. As president years later, Clinton would choose Reich to

Bill Clinton with a group of fellow students at Oxford University in 1968 during his two years as a Rhodes Scholar.

serve as his secretary of labor. Other fellow Rhodes Scholars also served in his administration.

Of the great issues of the day, the one that weighed heaviest on the minds of the young Americans, was the war in Vietnam. The government of South Vietnam had been fighting the Vietcong, guerrilla fighters supported by Communist North Vietnam, since 1958. Then in 1964, President Lyndon B. Johnson began sending U.S. combat troops to support the South. By 1968, more than 500,000 U.S. troops were stationed in Vietnam. U.S. and South Vietnamese troops had better weapons, including a powerful air force for bombing enemy positions, but they could not gain the upper hand in the dense jungles against the determined guerrillas. More than 30,000 U.S. troops and hundreds of thousands of Vietnamese had been killed, and there was no end in sight. At home, more and more Americans were asking if the war was worth the huge costs.

During the buildup of U.S. troops in Vietnam, the government began *drafting* young men for service in the U.S. military. Those required to serve were called up by local draft boards. For thousands who shared Clinton's belief that U.S. involvement in Vietnam was wrong, the draft created a terrible choice. If they were drafted, should they agree to fight in Vietnam for a cause they opposed? Or should they resist the draft and risk being sent to prison?

During his years at Georgetown, Bill Clinton and other college students had student *deferments* that postponed the draft until they finished their study. By the time he became a Rhodes Scholar, student deferments had been changed and only protected a student until the end of the current school term. Clinton received the dreaded call-up notice in April 1969 and was expected to report for induction at the end of the term, in May.

Several of Clinton's friends refused to serve. Yet this was not an option he considered. Clinton had settled on a career of government service. If he resisted

Few years in U.S. history have seen as much turmoil as 1968. Late in January, Vietcong and North Vietnamese troops attacked more than a hundred towns and fired shells into Saigon, South Vietnam's capital. The offensive was defeated, but it convinced many in the United States that the war could not be won.

On March 31, in a televised speech to the nation, President Johnson announced new efforts to make peace in Vietnam. Then he shocked the nation by announcing that he would not run for another term as president.

President Lyndon B. Johnson speaks to the nation on March 31, 1968. Under serious pressure by opponents of the Vietnam War, he announced that he would not run that fall for another term as president.

On April 4, civil rights leader Martin Luther King Jr. was shot and killed by an assassin. Angry African-Americans rioted in American cities. On June 5, Senator Robert F. Kennedy, brother of the slain president, won the Democratic presidential primary in California, but late that night, he too was shot and killed by an assassin.

In August, Democrats met in Chicago to nominate their presidential candidate, choosing Johnson's vice president, Hubert Humphrey. That news was overshadowed, however, by brutal clashes between thousands of antiwar protesters and Chicago police outside the convention hall. In November, Humphrey, a supporter of Johnson's war policy, lost the election to Republican Richard Nixon.

To many Americans, it seemed that the United States was going violently insane. Some turned to further violence, and others dropped out, not bothering even to vote. The events of 1968 shook Bill Clinton too, but he never lost his faith in the U.S. political system.

the draft, any ambitions to serve in public office would be finished. Clinton did try to avoid serving in Vietnam, however. To avoid reporting for induction, he arranged to enter the University of Arkansas Law School in the fall of 1969 and enter a military reserve unit. He would become a member of the military and train on weekends, but would be unlikely to be called up for duty in Vietnam. Then he had second thoughts. Instead of reporting to the University of Arkansas, he went back to Oxford for a second year of study.

Clinton might have been in trouble for "dodging" the draft, but a few months later, a further change in the draft law solved his problem. His chances of being drafted for Vietnam service evaporated. In the fall of 1970, he decided again against the University of Arkansas and enrolled at the law

Fast Facts

THE VIETNAM WAR

Who: The U.S. and South Vietnam against the Vietcong guerrillas and North Vietnam

When: Fighting began in the late 1950s; after 1964, U.S. involvement grew rapidly, reaching a height of nearly 550,000 troops by 1969. Beginning in 1970, President Nixon reduced U.S. troop strength and withdrew the last troops early in 1973.

Why: The Vietcong and North Vietnam wanted to unite Vietnam under Communist rule; the U.S. and its South Vietnamese allies wanted to keep Communists from taking over South Vietnam.

Where: South Vietnam and parts of neighboring Cambodia and Laos; military targets in North Vietnam were heavily bombed.

Outcome: An armistice signed in Paris in January 1973 brought a temporary halt to the fighting and ended U.S. involvement; in April 1975 Communist forces overran the South, and Vietnam was united under Communist rule. Fifteen years of fighting destroyed large regions of the country; at least 2 million Vietnamese fighters and civilians were killed; more than 58,000 Americans were killed.

school of Yale University. He was never drafted and never served in the military and his efforts to avoid wartime service would later haunt his political career.

Hillary ──────────────────────────────

In the fall of 1970, a bearded and bushy-haired Bill Clinton arrived at the Yale University Law School in New Haven, Connecticut, one of the top law schools in the country. As in his earlier studies, he excelled. "He was very quick," a house-mate later recalled. "I would love to know how fast he could read. He would get through more in an hour of concentrated effort than just about anybody I've ever seen. And he never slept much. If he slept more than four and a half hours a night, I'd be surprised."

Some at Yale were not as impressed, however. Clinton still spoke with a Southern accent, acted so friendly that some thought him phony, and had little money in his pockets. One biographer critical of the Clintons reported that Bill "was regarded by his classmates not as a future president but as a glad-handing hillbilly in floodwater pants."

One day, Clinton was talking to a friend in the law library while keeping his eye on a woman standing at the far end of the room. Finally, the woman approached. "If you're going to keep staring at me and I'm going to keep staring back, we ought to at least know each others' names. Mine's Hillary Rodham.

What's yours?" For once, Bill Clinton was speechless. He later joked that he had trouble blurting out his own name.

Hillary Rodham was an assertive young woman who grew up in a strongly Republican family in Illinois. Her conservative beliefs had been challenged by the Vietnam War, and she was influenced by an interest in *feminism*—a belief that women are fully entitled to lead independent lives, choosing a career over traditional roles as wife, mother, and homemaker. She too was a star student.

Bill and Hillary soon recognized how they complemented each other. While

Bill Clinton and Hillary Rodham in 1971 at the Yale Law School.

Bill was openhearted and easygoing, Hillary was more skeptical and disciplined. They shared high intelligence, ambition, and a strong belief that law, politics, and government could improve people's lives. Hillary's brilliance and sharp manner scared off many men, but Bill Clinton was intrigued. He didn't mind that she saw through his way of winning arguments by charming people or by tiring them out with long-winded arguments. "Come off it, Bill!" Hillary would say, and often he would stop. Gradually interest grew into romance, and soon these two strong-minded law students were a couple.

Return to Arkansas

In the summer of 1972, Bill and Hillary traveled to Texas. Bill was a manager of the state campaign for Democratic presidential candidate George McGovern, who was running against President Richard Nixon. Hillary worked on a voter-registration drive. McGovern, an early and outspoken opponent of the Vietnam War, was a hero to many young Democrats, but his beliefs were far more liberal than those of most voters. That November, he suffered one of the most crushing defeats in U.S. electoral history, and Nixon was easily re-elected.

Still, Bill Clinton came out of the campaign a winner. He already had a card file where he kept the names, addresses, and personal information about classmates, coworkers, and political organizers—anyone who might someday help with his political career. Now he expanded his file, using the Texas state Democratic mailing lists. "He learned from that race the power of a network," said a coworker. "McGovern didn't have [a network], and it hurt him."

In Clinton's own imagination, his future was taking shape. One day he spun out his dreams to Billie Carr, a talented Texas Democratic organizer. "I'm

In 1972 Clinton greets Democratic presidential candidate George McGovern at the Little Rock airport. Clinton spent the summer working on McGovern's campaign in Texas.

gonna tell you something and you're gonna laugh," he said. "As soon as I get out of school, I'm movin' back to Arkansas. I love Arkansas. I'm going back there to live. I'm gonna run for office there. And someday I'm gonna be governor. And then one day I'll be callin' ya, Billie, and tellin' ya I'm running for president and I need your help."

During their last year at Yale, Bill and Hillary agreed that their ambitions were diverging. He was intent on returning to Arkansas, but she wanted to launch her law career in the East. "I've got to go home. It's just who I am," he recalled telling her.

After graduation in 1973, the couple went their separate ways. Bill landed a teaching job at the University of Arkansas Law School, in the college town of Fayetteville. Hillary was soon called to Washington to help investigate the Watergate scandal, in which President Nixon and his aides were accused of abusing their power and covering up wrongdoing. (In August 1974, under threat of impeachment, President Nixon would resign as president.)

Before his first year of teaching ended, 27-year-old Bill Clinton announced his first run for public office—for a seat in the U.S. Congress from the 3rd District in Arkansas. He won the Democratic primary and faced the Republican congressman John Paul Hammerschmidt in November. Hammerschmidt was popular in the district, while Bill Clinton was scarcely known. Undaunted, Clinton used his charm and bottomless energy to raise his profile.

Clinton ran a brilliant campaign and was catching up to his experienced opponent, but it was not enough. He lost by 6,000 votes, only about 2 percent of the votes cast. He was disappointed, but tried to cheer his campaign workers: "We accomplished a miracle out here," he told them. "We started with no name recognition and look what we accomplished. We scared the pants off that guy."

The Boy Governor

Hillary came to Arkansas to help Bill with the unsuccessful 1974 House campaign. At Bill's urging, she accepted an appointment to the Arkansas Law School faculty. Bill and Hillary were back together, and Bill had told his mother, "It's Hillary or it's nobody." Still, there had been no promises, and the couple's future was still in doubt.

One day when Hillary returned to Fayetteville after a trip, Bill picked her up at the airport and drove her past a red-brick cottage that she had admired. "Remember that little house?" he asked. "I bought it. You have to marry me now, because I can't live there alone." Later that year, on October 11, 1975, they were married in the living room of that house. Like a growing number of young brides at the time, Hillary Rodham chose to keep her own last name.

Clinton had lost his first election, but he was a rising political star. In 1976 he was encouraged to run for attorney general, the state officer who provides legal advice and representation for the state. No Republican ran against Clinton, so he had the free time to direct the state campaign to elect Democrat Jimmy Carter for president. Both Carter and Clinton were elected. Bill and Hillary moved to Little Rock, the state capital. Hillary took a position with the Rose Law Firm, one of most influential law practices in the state.

Clinton worked hard as attorney general, but he saw the position as a stepping-stone. In 1978 he announced he would run for governor. That campaign demonstrated his talents as a campaigner. "He thrives on handshaking and elbow-rubbing that are the backbone of politics in Arkansas, and people bask in the warmth," noted political writer David Osborne. "Rather than wearing him down, the personal contact seems to rev him up. He is as comfortable and natural telling jokes with the good ol' boys as [he is] discussing international economic problems with a group of professors." Arkansas rewarded his hard work with 63 percent of the vote. Just 32, Bill Clinton had become the youngest governor of a U.S. state in 40 years.

Winning was a big step, but governing proved a much bigger challenge. Young and idealistic, Clinton moved aggressively to introduce new policies to his

Clinton is sworn in as the youngest state governor in 40 years in January 1979. Hillary is at the left.

state. Arkansas was one of the poorest states in the nation. The state government was deep in debt, and its educational system was one of the poorest. Unemployment was high, and out-of-staters saw Arkansas as the home of "hillbillies," uneducated mountain people.

Clinton pushed for education reforms. He worked to control clear-cutting of the state's forests by timber companies, and he fought for a plan to improve that state's sadly run-down highways. To pay for highway repairs, he persuaded the legislature to raise license fees on cars. Each of these actions angered some important group. The car license fees were especially unpopular. Clinton and his young staff lacked the experience to sell their new ideas to voters. When he was criticized, the governor sometimes tried to deny responsibility or shift blame to others, and this often backfired. One Arkansas newspaperman called the governor "Slick Willie," a nickname Clinton despised but could never quite leave behind.

One of the few happy things for the Clintons in 1980 was the birth of their daughter. Chelsea Clinton was born on February 27.

In April 1980, Fidel Castro, the Communist leader of Cuba, announced that anyone who was unhappy in Cuba (including some in prisons and mental hospitals) was free to leave the country. In the next six months, nearly 125,000 Cubans arrived in Florida on small boats, hoping to begin a new life in the United

Bill and Hillary with their baby daughter Chelsea in 1980.

States. They were sent to resettlement camps in various parts of the United States. One of the largest was at Fort Chaffee in western Arkansas, which received about 19,000 Cubans for processing.

On June 1, 1980, a group of refugees at Fort Chaffee rioted, and about 300 escaped, causing alarm in the small towns near the base. Governor Clinton was forced to call out the National Guard to help round up the escapees and to protect them from angry Arkansans who resented their presence. The images of chaos at Fort Chaffee shocked voters and made Clinton look like a weak leader who could not protect his state. Later that summer, President Carter announced that Fort Chaffee would become a permanent relocation center for even more Cuban boat people.

That November, Clinton was up for re-election. The Republican candidate, Frank White, ran negative ads hammering Clinton's record and his character. Critics even chided Hillary Rodham for not changing her last name when she married Clinton. At the same time, other problems assaulted the state. A drought damaged crops, and livestock were dying for lack of food. The state could not afford to offer much aid.

"Every time you turned around, there was a disaster," Clinton aide Patty Howe Criner recalled. "Chickens were dying, cows were starving, a terrible drought, Cuban refugees, and the car [license fee] issue."

On election day, Democrats wore gloomy faces in Little Rock and in Washington. Republican Frank White defeated Clinton for governor in a tight race. That same day, Republican Ronald Reagan defeated Jimmy Carter for president. "The loss stung Clinton badly," commented David Osborne. "But it taught him a fundamental lesson: that a reformer must find a way to do what his constituents want, not what he thinks they need."

Rise of the Comeback Kid

Electoral politics was not a job but a calling for Bill Clinton. He loved the campaigning, the attention, and the chance to exercise power to do good. No other career ever tempted him. After his defeat, he joined a law office, but his eyes were already on a 1982 rematch with Governor White. He called Betsey Wright, a skilled political organizer, to help organize his efforts. He also hired Dick Morris, a brash political strategist. Morris was helping revolutionize politics by using polls—a series of questions posed to potential voters—to measure the popularity of candidates and issues.

To launch Clinton's 1982 effort, Morris suggested that Clinton make a television ad apologizing for the mistakes he had made in his first term. Clinton hesitantly agreed. In the ad, he mentioned the unpopular policies from his term as governor and apologized to anyone who had been hurt by them. Then he added his own homespun appeal: "When I was a boy growing up, my daddy never had to whip me twice for the same thing. And now I hope you'll give me another chance to serve as governor because our state has many problems and opportunities that demand strong leadership."

The apology worked. Later criticisms glanced off because Clinton had already admitted his mistakes. To blunt attacks from conservatives, Hillary Rodham even reconsidered her name and changed it to Hillary Clinton. On election day, Clinton easily defeated Frank White, with 430,000 votes to White's 357,000. He had recaptured the governor's mansion, and his political career was back on track.

From that comeback the Clinton team developed three strategies that would guide his future campaigns. First, respond aggressively to attack ads. "When someone is beating you over the head with a hammer, don't sit there and take it," Clinton once said. "Take out a meat cleaver and cut off their hand." Second, don't rely on the press to deliver your message about achievements, plans, and policies. Pay for radio and television ads as well as mailings to reach voters directly. And third, use frequent polling to find out what people are thinking. "You can't lead without listening," was one of Clinton's themes during the 1982 race. Many future candidates would use these rules to help them win elections.

The Clintons exult in Bill's re-election as Arkansas governor in November 1982.

Once back in office, Clinton put most of his energies into educational reform. Arkansas teachers were terribly underpaid compared to teachers in other states. Many students graduated from underfunded schools unprepared for college or better-paying jobs. With poorly educated workers, Clinton argued, Arkansas would have an uphill battle attracting businesses and jobs to the state.

Clinton named Hillary, who had a strong background in education issues, to head the Education Standards Committee. The group found that the state's schools needed a complete overhaul. Among other shortcomings, 148 high schools had no physics classes, 180 had no foreign languages, and 204 had no music programs.

To pay for the plan, Clinton made a passionate plea for a tax increase of $180 million. He also called for required tests for teachers to make sure that they were qualified. He called these tests "a small price to pay for the biggest tax increase for education in the history of the state." The proposed tests enraged the Arkansas Teachers Association. It said that testing insulted the teaching profession. Teachers spent the next years trying to oust Clinton from office. Clinton's polls told him that voters approved of the tests, and he held firm. The teachers reluctantly took the tests. Later they admitted that Clinton's reforms had greatly improved education in the state.

The education reforms took hold over the next four years. Teacher pay increased. Physics, advanced math, and foreign languages became available in all districts. Limits were set on the number of students per class. The percentage of graduating seniors going on to college rose from 38 to 50 percent. The popularity of Bill Clinton, now known as the "education governor," also rose.

The state's economy improved throughout the 1980s, with unemployment dropping from 12 percent to less than 7 percent between 1983 and 1990. Voters overwhelmingly re-elected Clinton in 1984. In 1986 Arkansas law was changed to increase the governor's term from two years to four years, and voters elected Clinton to the first four-year term. National leaders in the Democratic party began to take notice.

Going National

In a letter to fellow Rhodes Scholars in 1986, Robert Reich wrote, "Rumor has it that Bill [Clinton] will be the Democratic candidate for president in 1988. I just made up that rumor, but by the time you read this, the rumor will have spread to the ends of the nation."

Reich had reason to predict a presidential race. Clinton was already active in national Democratic politics. He gave speeches at the Democratic conventions

Clinton speaks at the 1988 Democratic convention to nominate Governor Michael Dukakis for president.

in 1980 and 1984. He was chosen chairman of the National Governors Association in 1986. After his election in 1986, he briefly explored running for president in 1988, but decided that he was not ready and the time was not right.

The 1988 Democratic National Convention in Atlanta, Georgia, proved a low point of Bill Clinton's career. He delivered a nominating speech for presidential hopeful Michael Dukakis that made him look and sound like a hapless stooge. The lighting was bad, the sound system was poor, and the audience wasn't listening. Nonetheless, his speech seemed to go on and on. Afterward, his sense of humor came to his rescue. "It was the worst hour of my life—no make that hour and a half," he joked, even though the speech lasted only 32 minutes.

Michael Dukakis won the Democratic nomination, but was beaten soundly by Republican George H. W. Bush in November 1988. Bill Clinton was re-elected governor in 1990, and he began laying the groundwork for his own presidential run in 1992. On October 3, 1991, he stood on the steps of the Old State House in Little Rock, facing a crowd of 4,500. "I am declaring my candidacy for President of the United States," he told them.

Chapter 4

Comeback Kid, Part Two —————————

In 1990 Iraq invaded and occupied the neighboring country of Kuwait. When Iraqi leader Saddam Hussein refused to withdraw his troops, the United States and its allies gained United Nations support for military action. The allied forces began bombing Iraqi military targets in January 1991. In February, a large U.S.–led force drove Iraqi troops out of Kuwait in only four days. This quick victory sent the popularity of Republican president George H. W. Bush soaring. His re-election in 1992 seemed a sure bet.

At home, though, the U.S. economy was in trouble. During his 1988 presidential campaign, President Bush had promised to hold the line against raising taxes. "Read my lips," he said, "no new taxes." As the 1992 presidential campaign approached, a *recession*, or business slowdown, began, bringing higher unemployment and soaring govern-

Fast Facts

THE PERSIAN GULF WAR

Who: U.S.–led coalition against Iraq

When: January 17 to February 28, 1991

Why: Iraq invaded Kuwait, its oil-rich neighbor, in August 1990; the coalition formed to drive the Iraqis out of Kuwait.

Where: The Persian Gulf, Kuwait, and Iraq

Outcome: The coalition began bombing Iraqi military targets on January 17 and launched a major ground invasion in late February, driving Iraqi forces out of Kuwait and into southern Iraq in four days and nights of fighting. Iraq's Saddam Hussein agreed to destroy his "weapons of mass destruction" and allow United Nations inspections of military sites. About 380 coalition troops died and fewer than 1,000 were wounded. Between 25,000 and 75,000 Iraqis were killed.

ment *deficits* (the amounts by which yearly expenses are greater than income). Bush was forced to break his campaign promise and support tax increases to increase the government's income. The broken promise angered conservatives in his own party and endangered his re-election.

The Democrats, meanwhile, had no strong national leader. Nearly a dozen candidates entered the presidential primaries, seeking the presidential nomination. One of them was Bill Clinton. In his speeches, Clinton promised voters a "New Covenant" between government and the American people, offering more affordable health care, education reform, welfare reform, job training, middle-class tax relief, and government help in spurring the economy. He positioned himself as a moderate, balanced between the more conservative Republicans and his own party's liberals.

President George Bush campaigns with his wife Barbara on a campaign tour.

The first presidential primary was held in New Hampshire in mid-February 1992, and it was important for Clinton to do well there. Before the vote, however, rumors of scandal damaged Clinton's chances. Reporters suggested that Clinton had affairs with other women during his years as Arkansas governor, that he had dishonestly avoided military service during the Vietnam conflict, and that he might have been involved in crooked financial schemes.

Clinton's hopes seemed to be drowning in rumors, but he refused to surrender to such gossip. On January 26, 1992, he and Hillary appeared together on *60 Minutes*, a leading television news program. Addressing rumors of connections to other women, Clinton confessed to "causing pain in my marriage," but he refused to go into specifics. Hillary stood behind him. "I'm sitting here because I love him and I respect him and honor what he's been through and what we've been through together," she said. "And, you know, if that's not enough for the people, then heck, don't vote for him."

The national television appearance seemed to turn the tide. Three weeks later, Clinton finished a strong second in the New Hampshire primary behind Paul Tsongas, the governor of neighboring Massachusetts. It was the good showing he needed. He thanked voters, saying, "New Hampshire, tonight, has made Bill Clinton the Comeback Kid."

Clinton greets supporters in Merrimack, New Hampshire, on the night of the New Hampshire primary. After his encouraging showing, he called himself "the Comeback Kid."

In March, he swept eight Southern state primaries, and later took the crucial Midwestern states of Michigan and Illinois. He won the New York primary in April. In June, his victory in California assured him of the nomination. "Say what you want [about Clinton], but do not say that he quits," wrote New York columnist Jimmy Breslin.

Clinton accepted his nomination at the Democratic convention in New York City in July. He chose Tennessee senator Al Gore Jr. as his vice president and "Don't Stop Thinking About Tomorrow" as their campaign theme song. Now he faced the Republican incumbent, President George H. W. Bush, and a surprising third-party challenge. Early in 1992, H. Ross Perot, a quirky Texas billionaire, entered the race. Using his own money, Perot organized a powerful grassroots movement appealing to independent voters disgusted with both major parties. In his folksy Texas twang, Perot promised to bring the huge federal deficit under control, claiming that his actions would stimulate the economy and create a better business climate and more jobs.

The Bush campaign continued the drumbeat of negative stories about Clinton's past. It played up the president's experience—and Clinton's lack of experience—in foreign affairs. Clinton hammered at Bush's failure to manage the economy and his seeming lack of interest in the welfare of the average voter.

Al Gore and Bill Clinton receive cheers at the 1992 Democratic convention after being nominated for vice president and president.

"People have lost faith in the ability of government to change their lives for the better," he said.

On election day, the race split three ways. Although Ross Perot did not carry a single state, he received 19 percent of the vote. President Bush received 37 percent. With 43 percent, Bill Clinton won the presidency. In the electoral college Clinton received 378 votes to Bush's 168 and Perot's 0. At 46, Bill Clinton became the first U.S. president born during the baby boom after World War II, and the third-youngest president in U.S. history (after Theodore Roosevelt and John F. Kennedy).

"The Big Leagues" ———————————————

"The American people have summoned the change we celebrate today," President Clinton said in his inaugural address. January 20, 1993, was a frigid day on the steps of the U.S. Capitol, but Clinton delivered his address without an overcoat. "Yes, you, my fellow Americans, have forced the spring. Now, we must do the work the season demands."

The Clinton team seemed less than ready for its first tasks, however. Clinton's young staff was disorganized and sometimes seemed brash and sloppy. Many were as inexperienced in Washington as Clinton himself. At an early news conference, Clinton's boyish communications director, George Stephanopoulos, was treated roughly by the assembled reporters. Veteran reporter Helen Thomas greeted him afterward and said, "Welcome to the big leagues."

During its first months, the Clinton team fumbled on a number of fronts. In the most highly publicized event, more than 80 members of a religious sect in

Bill Clinton is sworn in as president on January 20, 1993. Chelsea Clinton is at the bottom left; Al Gore and Hillary Clinton are to the right of Clinton.

Waco, Texas, died in April 1993 after their compound was attacked by federal agents. Eight weeks earlier, four agents had been killed in a gunfight with sect members. After surrounding the sect's compound for 55 days, the agents finally attacked, using tear gas to drive men, women, and children from the buildings. Fires broke out in the buildings, however, and most of the sect members were

The Clinton Cabinet

Clinton's *cabinet* (heads of major government departments who act as advisers to the president) was the most diverse in U.S. history. Janet Reno was the first woman to serve as U.S. attorney general, the nation's highest law enforcement position. The cabinet also included African American Ronald H. Brown as secretary of commerce, and Latino Henry Cisneros as secretary of housing and urban development. In 1996, Clinton appointed Madeleine Albright as secretary of state. She was the first woman to serve as the nation's leading diplomat.

☆☆☆

killed. Some Americans were outraged that government agents had invaded a religious community; others were angry because the aggressive action had caused so many deaths. Some held Clinton's new attorney general, Janet Reno, responsible for the tragedy.

Still, the new president succeeded in a string of early actions. He signed the Family and Medical Leave Act into law, allowing workers to take up to 12 weeks of unpaid leave to care for a new baby without losing their jobs. In September 1993, Clinton established AmeriCorps, an organization especially dear to his heart. The program places thousands of volunteers in poor communities to teach or provide other needed services while they earn money for their

Clinton swears in a group of new volunteers joining AmeriCorps, the group he helped establish to provide teachers and other needed workers in poor communities.

education. In November, Clinton signed the Brady Handgun Violence Prevention Act. This gun-control measure required a five-day "cooling-off" period and a background check before someone could buy a handgun.

That December, Clinton worked with both Democrats and Republicans to pass the North American Free Trade Agreement (NAFTA). The plan, originated during the Bush administration, removed *tariffs*, or taxes, on trade between the United States, Canada, and Mexico. Critics warned that U.S. workers would lose their jobs when U.S. companies shifted their plants to Mexico where workers were paid less. Supporters claimed that in time, free trade would boost business and manufacturing for all.

Clinton also succeeded in passing a broad economic plan to increase the tax rate on wealthy Americans and cut government defense spending. Democratic majorities passed the plan in Congress without a single Republican vote. Republicans warned that higher taxes would cause a business slowdown, but the economy rebounded strongly. In addition, the government's new revenues helped reduce huge government deficits. Clinton later pointed to the 1993 economic package as one of the major achievements of his administration.

The Clinton administration had less success on its most ambitious proposal, the Health Security Act of 1993. At the time, more than 37 million Americans had no health insurance, making it difficult for them to get medical care. The Clinton plan called for a partnership between government and business to provide universal health care, guaranteeing medical coverage for all Americans. The act was written by a task force headed by Hillary Clinton, even though she had no official position in the government.

The Whitewater Scandal

The Clintons invested in the Whitewater project in 1978. The business did not do well, and it was broken up in 1992. The Clintons claimed to have lost $40,000 on their investment. There were many unanswered questions, however. Their partners in the project were James and Susan McDougal. James McDougal also owned Madison Guaranty Savings and Loan, a type of bank. After the savings and loan failed, investigators found evidence of illegal loans. Had the Clintons benefited from these? Had they bribed people to keep quiet about illegal actions?

In August 1994, Republican judge Kenneth Starr took over as special prosecutor. His aggressive investigation led to the conviction of the McDougals and Arkansas governor Jim Guy Tucker on charges related to the savings and loan business. Starr continued to expand his investigations as the months passed. At times he used threats and intimidation to get witnesses to confess and give evidence against the Clintons. Clinton viewed the Republican-backed investigation as a politically motivated witch-hunt designed to wreck his presidency.

In 2000, after six years of investigation, the Clintons were cleared of any charges in the Whitewater land deal. By that time, however, Kenneth Starr had uncovered other wrongdoing unrelated to Whitewater, which led to the impeachment of Bill Clinton.

☆ ☆ ☆

Special Prosecutor Kenneth Starr investigated the Whitewater scandal and later prepared the report on Clinton's actions that served as a basis for his impeachment.

The health care bill was energetically opposed by many of the groups most closely involved, including doctors' groups, insurance companies, and drug makers. They argued that the Clinton plan was too costly and would ruin the quality of U.S. health care. The campaign against the bill succeeded, and by September 1994 it was dead. Clinton never again proposed such a sweeping and ambitious plan. Instead, he would settle for smaller programs, smaller victories, and smaller defeats.

Even before the health care bill failed, Clinton was under fire for a private investment deal in his past. In the 1970s and 1980s, Bill and Hillary had been involved in a failed Arkansas real estate project called the Whitewater Development Corporation. Had they used their connections to make money unfairly? Or had they just made a bad investment? In January 1994, Clinton agreed to calls for a federal investigation of his Whitewater dealings.

In May 1994, there was more bad news. An Arkansas woman named Paula Jones filed a federal lawsuit accusing Clinton of sexually harassing her in 1991 when he was governor. Clinton denied the accusations, but they raised another question about his personal behavior. Adding grief to these troubles, his mother died early in 1994.

Perhaps the most severe setback for Clinton's presidency was the congressional election in 1994. Conservative Republicans, led by Georgia Representative

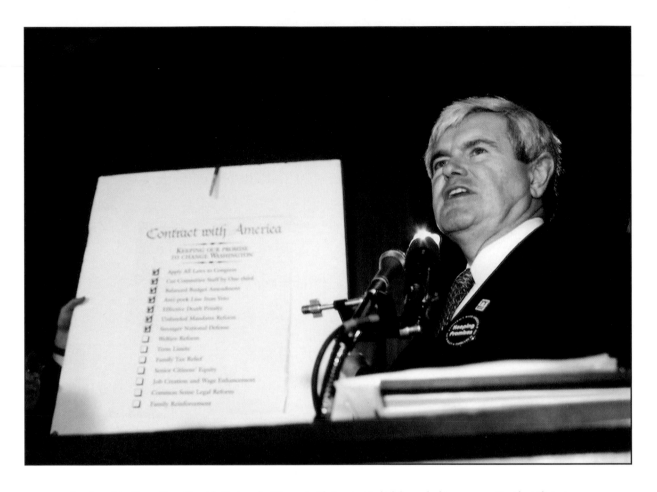

Speaker of the House Newt Gingrich displays the "Contract with America," which he worked to pass over President Clinton's objections.

Newt Gingrich, won *majorities*—more than half the seats—in both the House and Senate for the first time in 40 years. Gingrich himself was soon elected Speaker of the House. For the rest of his presidency, Clinton faced a Congress that opposed most of his proposals and attacked his leadership at any opportunity.

The Comeback Kid, Part Three

"Just keep going at them till they tire." That was Clinton's stock answer on dealing with a Republican Congress. The Republicans were determined to push through their own program, called the "Contract with America." Among its ten goals, the contract sought to reduce federal welfare programs, cut taxes, and reduce spending on domestic programs. Under Gingrich's leadership, the House passed many of these bills. The Senate proved less enthusiastic. It refused to vote on one measure and voted down others. Clinton *vetoed* one measure, refusing to sign it into law. Still, the "Contract with America" was widely popular, and Clinton's popularity sank to its lowest point.

Even though he began with little experience in foreign affairs, Clinton scored several diplomatic triumphs in his first term. In 1993, he helped negotiate an agreement between Israeli and Palestinian leaders in their long-running conflict in the Middle East. In 1994, with the help of former president Jimmy Carter, he forced a military dictatorship in Haiti to turn over power to the country's elected president. In 1995, he worked to forge a peace agreement that helped bring an end to a bloody civil war in Bosnia, a small country in Eastern Europe.

In April 1995, Clinton faced a searing tragedy at home when a truck bomb destroyed a federal office building in Oklahoma City, killing 168 people. He led the nation in grieving for the victims and providing comfort to their families. "You have lost too much, but you have not lost everything," he told the families. "And you have certainly not lost America, for we will stand with you for as many tomorrows as it takes." The bombers, who were protesting government actions at nearby Waco in 1993, were soon caught and were later convicted.

In late 1995, the White House and the Republican-controlled Congress deadlocked on negotiations about the federal budget—the plan for government spending in the coming year. Congress insisted on severe cuts in spending on many federal programs, but Clinton refused to agree. Seeking to pressure Clinton, Congress refused to appropriate money to run the government until a budget agreement could be reached.

The clash turned into a game of "chicken": which side would give in first? Twice, the budget crisis shut down the government, closing offices and cutting off paychecks to federal employees. Clinton insisted he was willing to compromise, but Congress stood firm on its demands.

Republicans expected that the government shutdowns would show Clinton in a bad light and help defeat him in the 1996 presidential campaign. As the crisis continued, however, citizens began to favor the president. Congress seemed petty and hard-hearted, insisting on big cuts in spending for Medicare

The National Air and Space Museum in Washington closes because of a government shutdown during the budget conflict between President Clinton and Congress.

and Medicaid—federal programs that pay for health care for senior citizens and poor people. Clinton emerged as a leader willing to battle for his beliefs. Congress and the president finally negotiated a compromise solution, but many saw Clinton as the winner of the battle.

In the summer of 1996, Republicans nominated Bob Dole, a longtime senator from Kansas, to run against Clinton in November. Despite Clinton's uneven record, Republicans found him a difficult candidate to run against. The economy was booming, unemployment was low, and most people were not in the mood to change administrations. Clinton won a second term with 49 percent of the vote to Dole's 41 percent. Ross Perot ran again as an independent, but received only 8 percent. In the electoral college, Clinton received 276 votes to Dole's 156. The one big disappointment for Clinton was the congressional races. Voters were happy with Clinton, but they also seemed happy with a Republican Congress, electing Republican majorities in the House and the Senate.

Chapter 5

Leading from the Center ———————

In January 1997, Bill Clinton took the oath of office for the second time. He had always been a moderate in his own party, endorsing some views of liberal and moderate Democrats. Now, forced into an uneasy partnership with a Republican Congress, he shifted even farther to the conservative side.

In his inaugural speech, he embraced the traditional Republican theme that the U.S. government had grown too big. He said:

> As times change, so government must change. We need a
> new government for a new century, humble enough not to
> try to solve all our problems for us, but strong enough to
> give us the tools to solve our problems for ourselves; a
> government that is smaller, lives within its means, and
> does more with less.

The speech echoed Clinton's earlier actions. In 1993 he had launched an initiative to "reinvent government," reducing its size and making it more efficient. By 1997, the program was showing results. Clinton had also addressed one of the largest government programs, payments of public assistance, or "welfare." In 1996 he had signed a bill to "end welfare as we know it." It required able-bodied people who received welfare payments to work, and limited the number of years they could receive welfare payments. Now, in May 1997, he led the drive for the Welfare to Work Partnership, a program to help more people get off welfare, get needed education and training, and find jobs.

The booming economy, reduced military spending, and Clinton's economic initiatives also helped continue dramatic reductions of the government's deficit. In his 1998 State of the Union address, he was able to tell Americans, "I will submit to Congress for 1999 the first balanced budget in thirty years."

Impeached

The Clinton ship of state seemed ready for smoother sailing, but a terrible storm was brewing. On January 21, 1998, a *Washington Post* headline proclaimed,

CLINTON ACCUSED OF URGING AIDE TO LIE;

STARR PROBES WHETHER PRESIDENT TOLD WOMAN

TO DENY ALLEGED AFFAIR . . .

The story reported that Clinton had been accused of having a sexual affair with Monica Lewinsky, a White House intern. Days earlier, Clinton had given a *deposition*, a legal statement given under oath to tell the truth, denying the relationship. At a press conference, he repeated his denials. "I did not have sexual relations with that woman, Ms. Lewinsky," he growled, jabbing a finger at reporters. "I never told anybody to lie, not a single time—never." His cabinet and Hillary defended him publicly.

The accusation would not die, however. Special Prosecutor Kenneth Starr

Monica Lewinsky, who served as an intern at the White House, appears to testify about her relationship with the president.

had expanded his investigation of the Whitewater affair to consider other legal violations. He now charged that President Clinton had carried on an "inappropriate relationship" with Monica Lewinsky, then had lied about it, committing the crime of *perjury*, lying while under oath to tell the truth. Faced with Starr's evidence, Clinton was forced to confess to his relationship with Lewinsky. On national television he apologized for his misconduct and for having "misled" his wife, his friends, and the public. He continued to deny, however, that he had lied in his deposition or that he had ever advised Monica Lewinsky to lie.

The scandal touched off a firestorm of debate. Newspapers, television news programs, magazines, and online news sources all reported on Clinton's behavior and his testimony. Some said he should resign to save his administration from further embarrassment. Some called for Congress to remove him from office. Clinton's supporters believed that his enemies were trying to destroy him over a matter that did not affect his actions as president.

Even without further legal action, the scandal damaged the president. Those who had defended his earlier statements were angry. Hillary, who had believed his denial of a relationship with Monica Lewinsky, was furious. Chelsea, now a student at Stanford University in California, was deeply embarrassed. In addition, millions of Americans no longer trusted Clinton's word.

Meanwhile, the House of Representatives voted to begin an investigation to determine if Clinton should be *impeached*—whether they should charge the president with "high crimes and misdemeanors." If a majority of the House voted to bring impeachment charges, Clinton would be tried with the Senate serving as the jury. If the Senate decided by a two-thirds majority that Clinton was guilty of any charge, he would be convicted and removed from office.

President Clinton on August 17, 1998, just before admitting on television that his relationship with Monica Lewinsky was "not appropriate."

Hot words flew between Republicans and Democrats as the impeachment vote approached in the House. Illinois Republican Henry Hyde spoke in favor of impeachment. "The question . . . is rather simple," he said. "It's not a question of sex. . . . It's not even a question of lying about sex. The matter before the House is a question of lying under oath. This is a public act, not a private act. This is called perjury. "

Democrat Jerry Nadler of New York responded. "Perjury on a private matter, perjury regarding sex, is not a great and dangerous offense against the nation," he said. "It is not an abuse of uniquely presidential power. It does not threaten our form of government. It is not an impeachable offense."

In December, the full House passed two articles of impeachment. Nearly all Republicans voted in favor of the articles, and nearly all Democrats voted against them. The impeachment trial of the president began on January 7, 1999. The Chief Justice of the United States served as presiding judge; the Senate sat as a jury; and House members served as prosecutors. The president was represented by his own attorneys.

Bill Clinton continued to perform his presidential duties, trying to show that he was calm and in control. His approval ratings remained very high. Most Americans were disappointed in his behavior and his failure to tell the truth. At

President Clinton delivers his State of the Union address to Congress on January 19, 1999. Even though his impeachment trial had begun, Clinton stressed that the state of the Union was "strong."

the same time, they approved of his conduct as president. Many believed that the impeachment was all about politics.

In the middle of the trial, on January 19, 1999, Clinton delivered his State of the Union address to both houses of Congress. He said nothing about the charges or the trial. Instead, he described how well the country was doing:

For the first time in three decades, the budget is balanced. . . . Thanks to the pioneering leadership of all of you, we have the lowest crime rate in a quarter century and the cleanest environment in a quarter century. America is a strong force for peace. . . . My fellow Americans, I stand before you tonight to report that the state of our Union—is strong.

After more than a month of testimony and lawyerly debate, the Senate voted on the impeachment of William Jefferson Clinton on February 12, 1999. To convict and remove him from office, 67 votes were required. On the first article, charging that Clinton had committed perjury, 45 senators voted "guilty" and 55 voted "not guilty." On the second article, charging that Clinton had obstructed justice, 50 senators voted "guilty" and 50 voted "not guilty." The Senate had *acquitted*, or cleared, President Clinton of the impeachment charges.

Bill Clinton was only the third president in U.S. history to be threatened with removal from office through impeachment. The first was President Andrew Johnson. In 1867 a hostile Republican Congress brought charges against him, charging that he ignored a law Congress had recently passed to reduce presidential authority. The House voted to impeach, and Johnson was tried. A majority of the Senate voted to convict him, but the vote was one short of the required two-thirds majority. Johnson served the remainder of his term.

On February 12, 1999, the U.S. Senate votes on the articles of impeachment against President Clinton. They acquitted him on both articles.

In 1974 the Judiciary Committee of the House of Representatives approved three articles of impeachment against President Richard Nixon for his actions in the Watergate scandal. Nixon, faced with evidence that the full House would vote to impeach him and that the Senate would convict him, resigned the presidency on August 9, 1974. The remainder of his term was served by Gerald Ford.

☆ ★ ☆

Lame Duck

President Clinton still had nearly two years left in office following the impeachment trial. As a "lame duck" president, however, his power was greatly reduced. Since he was serving his second term as president, he could not run again in 2000. This meant that the hostile Republican Congress could defeat or stall any of his proposals, hoping that a Republican president would replace him in the 2000 election. Like a duck with an injured wing, he had lost a vital part of his power. Clinton's only consolation was that he still had broad public support. In 2000, the year after his impeachment, his approval rating in opinion polls reached 65 percent, the highest figure for any president during his final year in office.

Clinton continued to exercise his remaining executive power. In 1999, officials in Yugoslavia had mounted an offensive against residents of Kosovo, a territory of Serbia. As thousands of Kosovars were driven out of their cities, Clinton gathered support from allies in the North Atlantic Treaty Organization (NATO) for a bombing campaign to end the violence. With congressional approval, the United States led the 79 days of air attacks, until the Serbian government agreed to end its campaign. The United Nations then sent in peacekeeping troops to aid Kosovar refugees in returning to their homes.

At home, President Clinton signed executive orders creating national monuments to protect unique sites on federal land. He pushed for more federal funds to pay for after-school and summer school programs and for school repairs. He used the "bully pulpit"—his prestige and authority as president—to ask Americans to contribute more public service and seek ways to ease racial tensions.

One major goal eluded him. As his second term neared its end, U.S.–guided talks to bring peace between Israel and the Palestinians broke down. Before long, violence between the two sides resumed.

By mid-2000, Clinton began to shift to the background. He and Hillary had bought a home in Chappaqua, New York, to live in after they left the White House. In July, Hillary announced that she would run for the U.S. Senate from New York in the fall elections. Early in August, Texas governor George W. Bush, the son of President George H. W. Bush, accepted the Republican nomination for president. Later that month, Clinton's vice president, Al Gore, accepted the Democratic nomination. From then on, attention focused on the campaigns, and the lame duck president was left out. Even though Clinton remained popular, millions of voters despised him, and he was not invited to campaign.

The presidential election of 2000 was one of the closest and most controversial in U.S. history. On election night, television networks first projected that Gore was elected, then withdrew their projection and termed the race "too close to call." In the final tally, Gore received about 500,000 more votes than George

During the Clinton years, Al Gore established himself as one of the most active vice presidents in U.S. history. He was regularly included in administration planning and headed the "reinventing government" program that streamlined the federal government. He also helped rally public support for the North American Free Trade Agreement (NAFTA) and used his special expertise on the development of the Internet and on environmental policy.

President Clinton and Vice President Gore raising funds for Gore's 2000 campaign for president.

Before serving as vice president, Gore had served in the U.S. House and the U.S. Senate, following in the footsteps of his father, Albert Gore Sr. As the Democratic candidate for president in 2000, Gore faced a difficult challenge. He lacked the charm and easy manner of President Clinton, and he ran in a heated political atmosphere still inflamed by the Clinton impeachment. He lost the presidency to George W. Bush in a disputed election that caused further bitterness between the two parties.

★★★

First Lady Hillary Rodham Clinton

Hillary Clinton was the most visible and active first lady since her hero, Eleanor Roosevelt.

Lawyer, child advocate, law professor, public policy expert, mother, author, and U.S. senator, she challenged the traditionally limited role of first lady. She traveled around the world encouraging women to make their presence felt in politics and government. In a 1997 speech to an international women's conference, she said, "There cannot be true democracy unless women's voices are heard. There cannot be true democracy unless women are given the opportunity to take responsibility for their own lives."

Traditionalists deplored Hillary Clinton's brand of feminism. At the same time, her outspoken views and political success won her many admirers and encouraged countless younger women to strive for challenging careers and to enter public service.

Senator Clinton speaks during a congressional hearing in 2004.

☆ ☆ ☆

On election night in November 2000, Hillary Clinton and her family celebrate her election to the U.S. Senate from New York.

Bush, but it appeared that Bush had won the election in the electoral college, 271 to 266. The outcome depended on which candidate won the most votes in Florida, where Bush led by barely 500 votes. Democrats challenged the vote there and demanded a recount. After weeks of court challenges, the U.S. Supreme Court ordered an end to recounting. Florida officials declared George W. Bush the winner in that state, and he won the election. For the Clinton family, there was a victory in the midst of disappointment. Hillary Clinton had been elected to the U.S. Senate from New York by a wide margin.

In January 2001, Bill and Hillary Clinton left the White House for their new residence in Chappaqua, 35 miles (56 kilometers) north of New York City. Hillary divided her time between New York and Washington, where she took her seat in the Senate. Bill set up an office of his own in New York City's Harlem. There he wrote his memoirs, published in 2004, and worked on plans for his presidential library in Little Rock. Admired by millions and condemned by millions, he remained one of the most controversial figures in modern U.S. politics.

Chapter 6

Time Will Tell ————————————

It is difficult to judge a presidency until many years after it ends. Only then can historians see the long-term effects of a president's policies and actions. It is especially difficult to judge Bill Clinton's. Few presidents have stirred more conflicting emotions. "I've never seen a person who draws such love and such hate," observed Beckie Moore, executive director of the Clinton Birthplace Foundation in Arkansas.

Clinton's abilities as a politician were beyond question. "This was an enormously talented man, one of the most talented people we've had in the Oval Office in the last 100 years, and gifted in so many ways," wrote journalist David Gergen, who had served in both Republican and Democratic administrations. "And he had a passion for change and improving people's lives, and using the government as a vehicle to do that."

Others have not been so generous. Even Clinton's old friend and labor secretary, Robert Reich, wrote, "The first post-Cold-War presidency could never find its point. Bill Clinton occasionally tried to tell us, but he wasn't bold enough or consistent enough; he seemed to compromise and weasel too much, and thus America never trusted him enough."

As president, Clinton never accomplished a landmark achievement such as Franklin Roosevelt's reshaping of the government during the Great Depression or Ronald Reagan's conservative revolution in the 1980s. In his one effort to accomplish a major change, achieving universal health care, Clinton failed to get his proposal passed by Congress.

Clinton's legacy will be measured by less dramatic initiatives in four main areas: his use of the "endless campaign," his influence on the Democratic party, his efforts to change the U.S. role in the world; and his contributions to economic growth.

The Endless Campaign ───────────────

After his defeat in his 1980 re-election bid for governor, Bill Clinton developed a new political strategy. He had found that voters remembered his mistakes but could not recall the good things he had done. News reporters would always be ready to criticize his mistakes, but could he count on them to report his successes or publicize a new policy or program?

The "endless campaign" was Clinton's answer to this question. When he returned as Arkansas governor, Clinton concentrated on telling people what he was doing—with an emphasis on the good things. To promote a program, he organized a campaign that included radio and television ads and mail direct to voters' mailboxes. With this strategy, he built statewide support for the program.

He carried the endless campaign into the presidency. Using cable news channels and the Internet as well as newspapers, network television, and mail, his team became expert at getting his message out. They also "listened," using public opinion polls to learn what people were concerned about, what they knew, and what they disliked.

Clinton's opponents soon followed his model. They too used every means of communication to get their message out—including their opposition to Clinton and his policies. The endless campaign often became a cycle of ugly attacks and counterattacks. Internet sites about Clinton continued to be deeply *polarized*, divided between those that revered him and those that despised him. Very few reported on his presidency or personality in a balanced way.

Bill Clinton with advisers George Stephanopoulos (left) and James Carville (center), part of the team that helped carry on his "endless campaign."

Leading Democrats on the "Third Way" ——

During the 1980s, Republicans successfully made the word "liberal" a dirty word in politics, and they used it against their Democratic opponents. According to Republicans, liberals wanted the government to do too much, be too big, and try to solve problems that people should solve themselves. They wanted to raise taxes and spend too much. Liberals were also viewed as soft on crime, reluctant to use military power, and too generous with government assistance.

Recognizing this, Clinton directed Democrats away from their liberal beliefs to a middle path that he called "the Third Way." "Government is not the problem, and government is not the solution," he said in his second inaugural address. His "reinventing government" initiative aimed to reduce government size and spending by cutting out wasteful practices. By 2000, the Clinton administration announced that it had cut 377,000 federal jobs and sharply reduced federal spending. In 1999, those reductions contributed to the first federal budget surplus in 30 years. In other words, more money came in from taxes than was spent by the government.

Clinton took other issues from the Republican playbook. He reformed welfare to limit how long people could collect payments. He cracked down on crime, successfully sponsoring federal funding that put 100,000 more police officers on U.S. streets. The rate of violent crime dropped. He endorsed the North American Free Trade Agreement initiated by President George H. W. Bush and helped get it adopted. Later he signed other free trade agreements.

His eagerness to find middle ground caused older Democrats to ask if Bill Clinton had any firm beliefs. He did support gun control, abortion rights, and rights for gays and lesbians, outraging many conservatives. Yet Democrats often opposed the conservative positions he adopted, including free trade and welfare reform.

One Superpower

When Clinton took office, the United States was still getting used to a new international order. After more than 40 years of rivalry between the United States and the Soviet Union, the Soviet Union had collapsed, leaving the United States as the only superpower. How would the United States use this new position as undisputed world leader? Clinton and his advisers wrestled with the problem.

At the same time, modern telecommunications and computers were rapidly changing international relations and business. A political or economic crisis in any part of the world could upset world markets and governments. This instant communication made the world a smaller place, but it also presented huge challenges. Bill Clinton learned to use U.S. economic, diplomatic, and military power effectively to influence this increasingly linked world.

Bill Clinton in the Oval Office.

In 1994 and 1995, Mexico faced a serious financial crisis. Clinton worried that the crisis would create an international recession and might even send thousands of unemployed Mexican workers across the U.S. border to seek jobs. He used his emergency powers to lend Mexico $20 billion. The loan stabilized the Mexican economy and was soon repaid. In 1998, he dealt with another financial crisis in Asia. He also used U.S. influence to provide debt relief to many poor countries so they could improve their living standards.

In military affairs, Clinton expanded the North Atlantic Treaty Alliance. Once an alliance of Western countries united against the threat of the Soviet Union, he helped refashion it into a wide alliance, encouraging former Communist countries—Poland, Hungary, and the Czech Republic—to join.

Clinton proved capable of taking action to stop trouble and violence in other world trouble spots. "Because the world is more connected every day and every way, America's security and prosperity require us to continue to lead in the world," he said in his farewell address.

Managing the U.S. Economy

"We began the new century with over 20 million new jobs, the fastest economic growth in 30 years, the lowest unemployment rates in 30 years, the lowest

The Rise of Terrorism

On February 26, 1993, a van filled with explosives blew up in the basement garage of the World Trade Center in New York City. Dense smoke filled one of the two towers, forcing thousands to evacuate. Six people were killed. In 1998, car bombs exploded outside two U.S. embassies in Africa, killing 224. In 2000, suicide bombers in a boat ripped a hole in the side of a U.S. Navy ship in Yemen, in the Middle East. The blast killed 17 U.S. sailors.

All of these terrorist attacks were linked to al Qaeda, an international terrorist organization which violently opposed the spread of U.S. influence in the world. As president, Bill Clinton took terrorism seriously, expanding the government's effort to identify terrorists and understand the threat. Twice he ordered air strikes to kill al Qaeda leaders, but the attacks failed. However, like most other political leaders at the time, he may not have recognized the full seriousness of terrorism.

On September 11, 2001, nine months after Clinton left office, al Qaeda terrorists shocked the world, when they hijacked four U.S. jets. They crashed two into the World Trade Center in New York City and one into the Pentagon, the headquarters of the U.S. military just outside Washington, D.C. The fourth plane, on its way to Washington, crashed in Pennsylvania. More than 3,000 people died. Terrorism took on new significance and sent U.S. foreign policy in a new and different direction.

Clinton and Secretary of the Treasury Robert Rubin, whose advice on the economy was important to Clinton's success.

poverty rates in 20 years," President Clinton said in his last State of the Union address. During his eight years as president, Bill Clinton oversaw the longest period of sustained economic growth in U.S. history.

How much did the Clinton administration contribute to the roaring U.S. economy of the 1990s? The U.S. economy is so complex that it is difficult to judge how much influence government leaders have. Still, Clinton and his economic advisers took an active hand in managing the economy. They succeeded in reining in government spending and keeping *interest rates* (the cost of borrowing money) low. This helped maintain business growth. By 1999, the federal deficit was replaced by a surplus, which contributed to business confidence.

A Mixed Report

Clinton served six of his eight years with a Republican-controlled Congress, a Congress that was openly hostile to him and his policies. In the past, this circumstance has led to gridlock, in which the government can't move in one direction or another. Clinton scaled back his ambitions, but he still accomplished many of his goals. He proved popular with average Americans, leaving office with the highest approval ratings of any modern president at the end of his term.

A clearer judgment of the Clinton years will be written years from now when historians have had a chance to compare his accomplishments to those of presidents who serve after him. The embarrassing chapters of scandal and impeachment will always mar his record. Yet his accomplishments during a period marked by peace and prosperity will always speak in his favor.

Fast Facts

William J. Clinton

Name at Birth:	William Jefferson Blythe IV
	(legally changed to William Jefferson Clinton in 1963)
Birth:	August 19, 1946
Birthplace:	Hope, Arkansas
Parents:	William J. Blythe III and Virginia Dell Cassidy Blythe
	Stepfather: Roger Clinton
Brothers & Sisters:	Half brother, Roger Clinton Jr. (1956–)
	Other half brothers and sisters fathered by W. J. Blythe III
Education:	Georgetown University, graduated 1968
	Rhodes Scholar, Oxford University, 1968–1970
	Yale Law School, graduated 1973
Occupation:	Attorney, law school instructor, elected official, author
Marriage:	To Hillary Rodham, October 11, 1975, in Fayetteville, Arkansas
Children:	(see First Lady Fast Facts at right)
Political Party:	Democratic
Public Offices:	1977–1979 Arkansas Attorney General
	1979–1981, 1983–1992 Governor of Arkansas
	1993–2001 42nd President of the United States
His Vice President:	Albert Arnold Gore Jr.
Major Actions as President:	1993 Signed the Family and Medical Leave Act
	1993 Signed Budget Deficit Reduction plan
	1993 Created the AmeriCorps community service program
	1993 Signed the Brady Handgun Violence Prevention Act
	1993 Signed the North American Free Trade Agreement
	1996 Enacted welfare reform
	1998 Balanced the federal budget for fiscal year 1999

Fast Facts

Hillary Diane Rodham Clinton

Birth:	October 26, 1947
Birthplace:	Chicago, Illinois
Parents:	Hugh and Dorothy Howell Rodham
Brothers & Sisters:	Hugh Rodham (1950–)
	Anthony Rodham (1954–)
Education:	Wellesley College, graduated 1969
	Yale Law School, graduated 1973
Occupation:	Attorney, public policy advocate, law school instructor, columnist, author, U.S. Senator
Marriage:	To William J. Clinton, October 11, 1975, in Fayetteville, Arkansas
Children:	Chelsea Victoria (1980–)
Political Party:	Democratic
Public Offices:	2001– U.S. Senator
Firsts:	Only president's wife to chair a federal government task force
	Only president's wife to win a Grammy Award (for recorded reading of her book *It Takes a Village*)
	Only president's wife elected to the U.S. Senate

Timeline

1946	1950	1963	1963	1964
William Jefferson Blythe III killed in car accident, May; his son, William Jefferson Blythe IV, born to Virginia Blythe, August 19	Bill's mother marries Roger Clinton, an automobile dealer	Bill legally changes last name to Clinton	Meets President John F. Kennedy, in Washington, D.C., July; Kennedy is assassinated, November	Gulf of Tonkin Resolution from U.S. Congress marks expansion of U.S. military action in Vietnam

1975	1976	1978	1980	1982
Marries Hillary Rodham	Elected attorney general of Arkansas	Elected governor of Arkansas	Daughter Chelsea Victoria is born; Clinton defeated for re-election as governor	Re-elected governor of Arkansas

1994	1995	1996	1998	1998
Independent counsel named to investigate Whitewater; mother dies; Republican majorities elected to both houses of Congress	Clinton vetoes Republican budget; budget crisis shuts down government twice; Federal Building in Oklahoma City bombed	Re-elected to second term as president; declares era of big government is over	First reports of Monica Lewinsky affair; U.S. embassies bombed in Kenya and Tanzania	House of Representatives votes to impeach Clinton on charges of perjury and obstruction of justice, December

1968	1970	1972	1973	1974
Clinton graduates from Georgetown University; wins a Rhodes Scholarship for study in England	Enters Yale Law School; meets Hillary Rodham	Assists Democrat George McGovern's presidential campaign in Texas	Earns law degree from Yale; Vietnam War ends	Defeated in election for U.S. House seat from Arkansas's Third District

1984	1986	1990	1992	1993
Re-elected governor	Re-elected governor for a four-year term; chosen chairman of National Governors Association	Re-elected governor	Elected 42nd president of the United States	Gains legislative successes with a Democrat-controlled Congress; brokers peace agreement between Israeli and Palestinian leaders

1999	2000	2001	2004
Senate acquits Clinton after impeachment trial, February; U.S. budget balanced for first time in 30 years; NATO bombs Serbian forces until they withdraw from Kosovo	Hillary Rodham Clinton elected senator from New York; George W. Bush defeats Vice President Al Gore in contested election	George W. Bush inaugurated; Clintons move to new home in Chappaqua, New York	Clinton publishes memoir, *My Life*

Glossary

acquit: the action of a jury or judge clearing an accused person of a crime or accusation

cabinet: the heads of U.S. government departments who meet to advise the president

deferment: a determination that an individual is not subject to being drafted for military service

deficit: the amount by which a government's yearly expenses are greater than its income

deposition: a legal statement for submission to a court, taken under an oath to tell the truth

diplomat: a government's representative to the government of another country

draft: a government program (usually in wartime) requiring some citizens to serve in the military

feminism: a belief that women are entitled to independence and may choose a career or profession over traditional roles as a wife, mother, and homemaker

impeach: to bring official charges of wrongdoing against a public official; the U.S. House of Representatives impeached Bill Clinton

interest rate: the cost of borrowing money, usually expressed as a percentage of the total amount to be paid each year

majority: more than half the seats in a legislature; the majority party often controls debate and is able to pass legislation it favors

perjury: the crime of telling a lie while under oath to tell the truth

polarized: divided between two extreme points of view

recession: an economic slowdown; business activity decreases and unemployment usually increases

tariff: a tax on goods brought into a country for sale

veto: the refusal of a president to sign into law a bill passed by Congress

Further Reading

Benson, Michael. *Bill Clinton*. Minneapolis, MN: Lerner Publications, 2003.

Cohen, Daniel. *The Impeachment of William Jefferson Clinton*. Brookfield, CT: Twenty-First Century Books, 2000.

Heinrichs, Ann. *William Jefferson Clinton*. Minneapolis, MN: Compass Point Books, 2002.

Kelly, Michael. *Bill Clinton*. Philadelphia: Chelsea House Publishers, 1999.

Levert, Suzanne. *Hillary Clinton*. Brookfield, CT: Millbrook Press, 1998.

Marcovitz, Hal. *Bill Clinton*. Broomall, PA: Mason Crest Publishers, 2003.

MORE ADVANCED READING

Allen, Charles F., and Jonathan Portis. *The Comeback Kid: The Life and Career of Bill Clinton*. New York: Birch Lane Press, 1992.

Clinton, Bill. *My Life*. New York: Knopf, 2004.

Clinton, Hillary Rodham. *Living History*. New York: Simon & Schuster, 2003.

Drew, Elizabeth. *On the Edge*. New York: Simon & Schuster, 1994.

Klein, Joe. *The Natural: The Misunderstood Presidency of Bill Clinton*. New York: Doubleday, 2002.

Levy, Peter B. *The Encyclopedia of the Clinton Presidency*. Westport, CT: Greenwood Press, 2002.

Maraniss, David. *First in His Class*. New York: Simon & Schuster, 1995.

Shogan, Robert. *Fate of the Union*. Boulder, CO: Westview Press, 1998.

Waldman, Michael. *POTUS Speaks*. New York: Simon & Schuster, 2000.

Places to Visit

★ ★ ★ ★ ★

Clinton Presidential Center
1200 President Clinton Avenue
Little Rock, AR 72201
(866) PRES-LIB (866-773-7542)
http://www.clintonpresidentialcenter.com/

On the banks of the Arkansas River in downtown Little Rock, the Clinton Center houses the largest collection of archived materials in presidential history.

Clinton Birthplace Foundation
117 South Hervey
Hope, AR 71801
(870) 777-4455
http://clintonbirthplace.org

For his first four years, Bill Clinton lived in this two-and-a-half story house with his grandparents.

"Clinton Loop" in Hope, Arkansas
Hope Tourist Center
Box 596
Hope, AR 71801
(800) 223-HOPE
http://www.americanpresidents.org/places/41b.asp

This tour visits sites related to President Clinton's early childhood in Hope, Arkansas.

"Clinton Loop" in Hot Springs, Arkansas
Hot Springs Convention and Visitors Bureau
Box K
Hot Springs, AR 71902
(800) 772-2489
http://www.americanpresidents.org/places/41c.asp

This driving tour visits Hot Springs sites connected to President Clinton's boyhood and teen years.

The White House
1600 Pennsylvania Avenue NW
Washington, DC 20500
Visitors' information line: (202) 456-7041

The Clinton family lived here from 1993 to 2001.

Online Sites of Interest

★ **The White House**

http://www.whitehouse.gov/history/presidents/bc42.html

Provides a brief biography of Bill Clinton. The site also provides information on the current president, biographies of other presidents, and information on timely topics of interest.

★ **The American President**

http://www.americanpresident.org/history/billclinton/

Provides valuable information on the life and times of U.S. presidents.

★ **Internet Public Library, Presidents of the United States (IPL POTUS)**

http://www.ipl.org/div/potus/wjclinton.html

Includes concise information about Clinton and his presidency; also provides links to other sites of interest.

★ **Presidents of the United States**

http://www.presidentsusa.net/clinton.html

Comprehensive site for presidential resources, including extensive biographical links.

★ **The American Presidency**

http://ap.grolier.com/

Provides biographical information on the presidents based on material in Scholastic/Grolier encyclopedias.

★ **CNN.Com In-Depth Special: The Clinton Years**

http://www.cnn.com/SPECIALS/2001/clinton/timelines/timelines.html

Comprehensive timeline of the Clinton presidency with analysis and interviews.

Table of Presidents

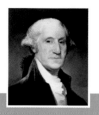   

1. George Washington **2. John Adams** **3. Thomas Jefferson** **4. James Madison**

	1. George Washington	2. John Adams	3. Thomas Jefferson	4. James Madison
Took office	Apr 30 1789	Mar 4 1797	Mar 4 1801	Mar 4 1809
Left office	Mar 3 1797	Mar 3 1801	Mar 3 1809	Mar 3 1817
Birthplace	Westmoreland Co, VA	Braintree, MA	Shadwell, VA	Port Conway, VA
Birth date	Feb 22 1732	Oct 20 1735	Apr 13 1743	Mar 16 1751
Death date	Dec 14 1799	July 4 1826	July 4 1826	June 28 1836

9. William H. Harrison **10. John Tyler** **11. James K. Polk** **12. Zachary Taylor**

	9. William H. Harrison	10. John Tyler	11. James K. Polk	12. Zachary Taylor
Took office	Mar 4 1841	Apr 6 1841	Mar 4 1845	Mar 5 1849
Left office	**Apr 4 1841•**	Mar 3 1845	Mar 3 1849	**July 9 1850•**
Birthplace	Berkeley, VA	Greenway, VA	Mecklenburg Co, NC	Barboursville, VA
Birth date	Feb 9 1773	Mar 29 1790	Nov 2 1795	Nov 24 1784
Death date	Apr 4 1841	Jan 18 1862	June 15 1849	July 9 1850

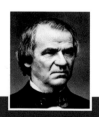  

17. Andrew Johnson **18. Ulysses S. Grant** **19. Rutherford B. Hayes** **20. James A. Garfield**

	17. Andrew Johnson	18. Ulysses S. Grant	19. Rutherford B. Hayes	20. James A. Garfield
Took office	Apr 15 1865	Mar 4 1869	Mar 5 1877	Mar 4 1881
Left office	Mar 3 1869	Mar 3 1877	Mar 3 1881	**Sept 19 1881•**
Birthplace	Raleigh, NC	Point Pleasant, OH	Delaware, OH	Orange, OH
Birth date	Dec 29 1808	Apr 27 1822	Oct 4 1822	Nov 19 1831
Death date	July 31 1875	July 23 1885	Jan 17 1893	Sept 19 1881

 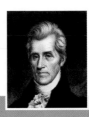 

5. James Monroe	**6. John Quincy Adams**	**7. Andrew Jackson**	**8. Martin Van Buren**
Mar 4 1817	Mar 4 1825	Mar 4 1829	Mar 4 1837
Mar 3 1825	Mar 3 1829	Mar 3 1837	Mar 3 1841
Westmoreland Co, VA	Braintree, MA	The Waxhaws, SC	Kinderhook, NY
Apr 28 1758	July 11 1767	Mar 15 1767	Dec 5 1782
July 4 1831	Feb 23 1848	June 8 1845	July 24 1862

13. Millard Fillmore	**14. Franklin Pierce**	**15. James Buchanan**	**16. Abraham Lincoln**
July 9 1850	Mar 4 1853	Mar 4 1857	Mar 4 1861
Mar 3 1853	Mar 3 1857	Mar 3 1861	**Apr 15 1865•**
Locke Township, NY	Hillsborough, NH	Cove Gap, PA	Hardin Co, KY
Jan 7 1800	Nov 23 1804	Apr 23 1791	Feb 12 1809
Mar 8 1874	Oct 8 1869	June 1 1868	Apr 15 1865

21. Chester A. Arthur	**22. Grover Cleveland**	**23. Benjamin Harrison**	**24. Grover Cleveland**
Sept 19 1881	Mar 4 1885	Mar 4 1889	Mar 4 1893
Mar 3 1885	Mar 3 1889	Mar 3 1893	Mar 3 1897
Fairfield, VT	Caldwell, NJ	North Bend, OH	Caldwell, NJ
Oct 5 1829	Mar 18 1837	Aug 20 1833	Mar 18 1837
Nov 18 1886	June 24 1908	Mar 13 1901	June 24 1908

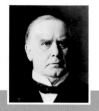

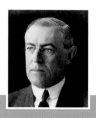

	25. William McKinley	**26. Theodore Roosevelt**	**27. William H. Taft**	**28. Woodrow Wilson**
Took office	Mar 4 1897	Sept 14 1901	Mar 4 1909	Mar 4 1913
Left office	**Sept 14 1901•**	Mar 3 1909	Mar 3 1913	Mar 3 1921
Birthplace	Niles, OH	New York, NY	Cincinnati, OH	Staunton, VA
Birth date	Jan 29 1843	Oct 27 1858	Sept 15 1857	Dec 28 1856
Death date	Sept 14 1901	Jan 6 1919	Mar 8 1930	Feb 3 1924

	33. Harry S. Truman	**34. Dwight D. Eisenhower**	**35. John F. Kennedy**	**36. Lyndon B. Johnson**
Took office	Apr 12 1945	Jan 20 1953	Jan 20 1961	Nov 22 1963
Left office	Jan 20 1953	Jan 20 1961	**Nov 22 1963•**	Jan 20 1969
Birthplace	Lamar, MO	Denison, TX	Brookline, MA	Johnson City, TX
Birth date	May 8 1884	Oct 14 1890	May 29 1917	Aug 27 1908
Death date	Dec 26 1972	Mar 28 1969	Nov 22 1963	Jan 22 1973

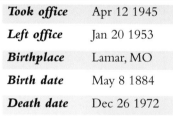

	41. George Bush	**42. Bill Clinton**	**43. George W. Bush**	
Took office	Jan 20 1989	Jan 20 1993	Jan 20 2001	
Left office	Jan 20 1993	Jan 20 2001	—	
Birthplace	Milton, MA	Hope, AR	New Haven, CT	
Birth date	June 12 1924	Aug 19 1946	July 6 1946	
Death date	—	—	—	

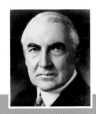			
29. Warren G. Harding	**30. Calvin Coolidge**	**31. Herbert Hoover**	**32. Franklin D. Roosevelt**
Mar 4 1921	Aug 2 1923	Mar 4 1929	Mar 4 1933
Aug 2 1923•	Mar 3 1929	Mar 3 1933	**Apr 12 1945•**
Blooming Grove, OH	Plymouth, VT	West Branch, IA	Hyde Park, NY
Nov 21 1865	July 4 1872	Aug 10 1874	Jan 30 1882
Aug 2 1923	Jan 5 1933	Oct 20 1964	Apr 12 1945

37. Richard M. Nixon	**38. Gerald R. Ford**	**39. Jimmy Carter**	**40. Ronald Reagan**
Jan 20 1969	Aug 9 1974	Jan 20 1977	Jan 20 1981
Aug 9 1974★	Jan 20 1977	Jan 20 1981	Jan 20 1989
Yorba Linda, CA	Omaha, NE	Plains, GA	Tampico, IL
Jan 9 1913	July 14 1913	Oct 1 1924	Feb 6 1911
Apr 22 1994	—	—	June 5 2004

• Indicates the president died while in office.

★ Richard Nixon resigned before his term expired.

Index

About the Author

Bill Clinton remains one of the most interesting political figures in the United States today, in the opinion of author Sean McCollum. Both Clinton and his wife Hillary have the ability to prompt passionate loyalty among supporters, and intense disapproval from critics. In writing this book, Sean found it challenging to track down fair-minded sources as he tried to present a balanced picture of the man and his presidency.

Sean thoroughly enjoys writing for young readers and learning along with them. A full-time freelance writer, he has published 15 books and hundreds of magazine articles. He loves travel, reading, running, and fretting about politics. Although he prefers his home in Colorado, he grew up in Minnesota and is a steadfast fan of the Vikings.

Photographs © 2005: AP/Wide World Photos: 73 (J. Scott Applewhite), 69 (Roberto Borea), 44, 80, 99 bottom (Ron Edmunds), 51 (Ron Frehm), 71, 98 bottom (Greg Gibson), 89 (Wilfredo Lee), 29, 41, 99 top right, 99 center left; Clinton Presidential Library: 8, 27, 35, 37, 57, 98 top, 98 center left, 98 center right 99 top center; Corbis Images: 55, 99 center right (Jacques M. Chenet), 59 (Win McNamee/Reuters), 78 (Jeff Mitchell/Reuters), 79 (Molly Riley/Reuters), 18, 99 top left (Bob Rowan/Progressive Images); Corbis SABA/Shepard Sherbell: 92; Corbis Sygma: 64 (Tom Horan), 61 (Jeffrey Markowitz), 14 (Art Meripol), 22 (Matthew Polak), 11 (Mike Stewart), 53 (Ira Wyman), 75; Getty Images/Dirck Halstead: back cover, 5; Index Stock Imagery/Ralf-Finn Hestoft: 49; John F. Kennedy Library: 16; LBJ Library Collection/Yoichi R. Okamoto: 24; Library of Congress via SODA: front cover, 3; Magnum Photos/Burt Glinn: 13; Time Life Pictures/Getty Images/Cynthia Johnson: 86.

Table of Presidents photographs copyright © 2005 Library of Congress, except for George W. Bush copyright © 2005 www.RightNews.com

Library Media Center
Gregory Heights School